AF316630

CONTENTS

Dedication iii

Acknowledgments vii

The Bottom Line...1

I'm Done 2

Soul Ties 5

Fragments of my dream..7

New 10

Upon Arrival 12

Touched 13

This Is Me 19

Impulse Happens 23

Repentance Answers...25

Orgasm 27

Cultured Sweetness 30

Free 33

The Art of Coming 35

My Essential Thing..39

FROM *Within* ME

DR. MARSHA C. PARRIS

Copyright © 2022 Marsha C. Parris
All rights reserved.
ISBN:

DEDICATION

To everyone trying to find their voice.
Simple: Don't look at others; just pull from within.
It's in you.
If you just open your mouth, it will flow out.

ACKNOWLEDGMENTS

To Jah, for His consistency in my life, and for bringing quiet to my heart concerning matters of the heart. For breathing into me creativity and bestowing boldness to open my mouth and speak. For calling me to the deep and giving me the strength to take the plunge. For this: I Write!

To my hubby Jarred for being there in more ways than I can count. Thanks, Papi! You added strength to me and allowed me space to create. My love relationship between you and God are interwoven in the tapestry of the rebirth of this work. I look forward to 'the more'.

To my daughters, Ajee, Nia and Abigail, thank you for always being my loyal groupies and ever-encouraging peeps. You listened to almost every one of my poems. Opened yours wide, squirmed, laughed, even cried. I know you learned a lot about me in the process because of the conversations that ensued and you have inspired me to keep going.

I think that family often has their bias and I'm amazing to them, but when others are also able to identify 'the real', no jealousy just love and rejoice when you rejoice it's a beautiful thing. Because of this I must say thank you to some people who I think would step to just about anyone who would step to me…you know who you are.

The Bottom Line

Purchased delivered sanctified commissioned
all of that is me.
All I had to do was one day believe
deep in my heart and
with power encourage say some words with the movement of my lips that
there was no greater love than the cross
there was no greater reality than the resurrection
there was no better way than eternal life.
Now come and join me
Just say it and believe it
he died He lives
I'm free
The bottom line is just for me
Jesus, it is he.

I'm Done

No
Stop it
Get off of me already
No, I don't want you
I don't need you either
Stop

You just want me to feel good with a bad thing
You just want to come up in here
and touch and feel and caress me
and make me feel dirty
Well no way.

Yeah that's it
You want me to feel bad
You enter in and get a little guilt trip going
Because you jacked me up
Well, I don't think so
You need to go
we've done this too long

You ain't no friend
You tell me the things I want to hear
when you know good and well
they're not true
You big fat liar
you dirty thief
you just want to steal
what's not yours

Alright, fine, I admit
I had a little time to waste
and so, you found a little use for me
I said I wouldn't, but I did
I said I couldn't, but I tried
I even blamed you for it
you were fulfilling purpose, but it just wasn't mine

This isn't me
You've come to mess up my field
my field of integrity
Trying to stare me off my pathway
My pathway of purity

So what, I used to do it
who really cares
I sure don't

You know, I am just real tired of this nature
and all your little tricks
I'm wising up, but you too stupid to see it

Like I said
I don't want you
and my heart is hard to your ways.

It's like I'm dead but alive
my eyes are closed
but I ain't never seen more clearly.
I know you and where you come from
You ain't no friend
I've had enough

I met a friend
and he showed me water and blood
it came from all over
his side, his head, his feet, his hands
Heck, that blood looked just like mine

I felt like we were one
It was something about the dip I took
In the water, through the Spirit
It was like I was new
Nothing old is on me
I'm brand spanking new
Way too new for you.

You just can't hang here
I don't want you
This world ain't enough
And I want more
I need more
You want to conform me
But I've been transformed
I was a refuge
But I got me some political asylum
A little transfiguration

You ain't no friend
I met me a friend
And you just betta step
Cause sin, don't live here
No mor

Soul Ties

History.
Stress release.
Connection.
Explosion.
I thought my motives were okay.
I never ever meant to get here.
It was just a one-shot deal
But I was unprepared for the way you make me feel.
I didn't understand the power of your touch.
The power of your words.
The power of your infusion.
You in me.
Me receiving you and everything about you deep within me.
I underestimated the power of you.
And now I feel guilty
But I don't feel guilty because I should feel guilty.
How confused and lost can I be?
Yet in the middle of it all I feel is like you found me and this feels so right,
yet I know….
It's the tearing, right?
You know… between the right and the wrong?
But the power that is attached to the feels of the humanness of me is so
strong,
yet my spirit is bloody and it's crying out.

I thought I wouldn't mind feeling this way about you
But I'm realizing
I don't want to feel this way… about you.
It feels good, as a matter of fact its captivating
and restricts the commonsense areas of my mind to function with clarity
and when I want to say no, I say yes.
When I want to walk away, I feel like I can't get enough. When I think of
you, time dissipates,
and the smell of you….. again, it captivates.
I'm trapped.

I want to feel this way about HIM.

I want Him to consume my thoughts, my every move
I want to feel this passion for Him first
Then maybe you'll be added –later.
When? I don't know.
I can't afford to keep doing things backward.
I have to say goodbye to the way you make me feel.
This connection you have to my soul
I can't.
I must offer it to Him
This transaction is for my life's purpose
He must be first. Him and Him alone.

Fragments of my dream

Fire and brimstone
Power water life
Resurrection
Judgement and restoration
Flowing love through Your blood
The gashes and holes in Your anatomy
Last night I died
At your altar

You're all I want
You're all I ever needed
Draw closer
For only dead men can see Your face
I'm dead…

Faith writings with literal meanings
Your word

The heavens open and I'm new like You
Pure and holy
Tried and true

The glory is Yours for you are awesome
I am revived

Draw close in Your presence
In your essence
They are for my lifeline and my character
My legacy

There's a touch unknown
That comes with a flame the singes
But doesn't scorch, doesn't leave me in burn degrees
Yet it purifies
And leaves me in levels of righteousness and holiness

I'm closer
My bush is burning
It won't stop
My soul is thirsty
Hungry for You
My stomach grumbles
Completely dissatisfied

I had worship and I'm drunk
Anointed by death, through death
And with death I live

You entered like the camel through the eye of the needle
Piercing but without force
I was
I am
Open to You
Com in
I trust You

I can share you
I must
Right after I'm right with you, after I see You
You see you've been good
I'm selfish because of who you have become to me
what you have done for and in me
and what you are doing

Tear down my negatives
Build up my positives
Rescue and reassess my character
Reprioritize my priorities
Go deep, deeper

I'm dancing, floating, dying, burning, glowing, and living
I see my light. Yes, light is come
Now I'm dead, I can see
Only dead men see Your face.

New

Black, bent, broken, beaten.
Bleeding from the cracked abrasions
On my lanky legs
Blackened knees
Discolored arms
And two-toned face

Who am i?
Am I who I was?

White robe flowing gracefully
Is what I see
The wings of a dove?
Is what I hear
The twigs with the lips of his face?
The life it brings
Is what I see, me?

New before creation created me
A nature of sin with the blood of royalty
A gentile, yet a Jew?

Who am I?
A I the new?

Puncture, rip and masticate
My hands
My side
My feet
Place on me love that I can
Taste… bittersweet.
Sweat like drops of blood

Engage me to think
Of my death
As my birth
My transfiguration

Give me a mirror
So that I can see
Thee
Not thee but me

Who am I?
Am I the who was?
Am I the who is too?
Am I Gentile and Jew?
Am I new?

Upon Arrival

Salivating
Overwhelmed
Frustrated
Holding in
Release
Hunger
Eyes wide and red
Bloodshot from unending desire
Spread thin
Spread open
One and the same
Needing you
Wanting you
Hurting hard
Hardly waiting
Rising to the occasion
The challenge
Engaged
Trembling
Wet - Supple
Tenderly righteous
Time is up
Upon arriving

Touched

(This is written in patois, but translation is in parentheses)

Bwoy mi ah tell yuh
(Let me say)
Me neva feel nuttin like dat before
(I have never felt anything like that before)
Mi close mi eye dem
(I close my eyes)
An a peer colors mi si
(and all I see are colors)
Beauty so unreal it mek mi smile suh deep
(beauty so unreal it makes me smile deeply)
And it gimi
(and it gives me)
Hope fi endure haadship and di loss of mi fren dem
(hope to endure hardship and the loss of my friends)
An mos of all, love
(and most of all love).

Mi neva feel nuttin like dat before
(I've never felt that before)
It mek mi knee dem woblely enuf fi buckle unda
(it makes my knees weak enough to buckle)
Mi feelins dem suh trang
(my feelings are so strong)
Dem confuse mi brainwaves
(they confuse my brain)
Allowin it fi gi mi
(allowing my brain to give me)
Misguided directions.

Have mi ah talk upside down words like
(I'm speaking things that make no sense like)
Mi love fi eat juice and sing a new dance
(I love to eat juice and sing a new dance)
Or
Mi hafi guh wash mi teeth dem and brush mi face
(I have to wash my teeth and brush my face)
Or
Eyes smile nuh, and mout… cry
(Eyes, please smile, and mouth… cry)!

It sweet yuh si, says mi brain
(My brain says, It is sweet)
Dat it tell mi mout
(That it tells my mouth)
An mi tongue and taase bud dem
(my tongue and taste buds)
Dem fi enjoy ah ting
(to enjoy it)
An suh mi salivate from mi mind's conceptive reaction (and so I salivate
from my mind's understanding)
All from dis one feelin
(All from this feeling).

An mi brain seh, hawt – beat!
(My brain tells my heart to beat)
Beat like yuh neva beat before
(Beat like you never have)
And timp haad
(and thump hard)
Like yuh waah fi buss open
(like you are gonna burst open)
Feel di excitement, di pleasure
(feel the excitement, the pleasure)
Be hapi and get likkle ecstasy
(Be happy and go higher)
Fluta
(flutter)

An mi brain jus a talk tuh mi loud lod
(my brain is so loud)
An it tell mi finga tip dem fi tingle
(it tells my fingertips to tingle)
An di hair dem pon mi kin tan up
(and the hairs on my skin raised)
Tan up at attention
(stand at attention)
Mek di win blow thru yuh
(lt the wind blow through you)
An gi yuh a chril
(and give you a thrill)
Feel dis ting man
(feel it)
It irie
(it's great)

Body, shake likkle
(shake a little body)
Han move
(hands move)
Han touch
(hands touch)
From di head tuh di toe
(from head to toe)
Wait wait wait
Duh mi a beg yuh
Hole on de likkle
(wait please, wait a minute please)
Mi sey a piece ah heat
(great heat)
Reach inna mi sections
(reached within me)
Wid no time fi corrections
(with no time for change)

It sweet yuh si
(it is so sweet)
Ah peer colors mi si
(all I see are colors; beauty)
Mi feel like mi caah help myself
(I feel like i'm out of control)
Don't know how fi hangle it
(I can't get a handle on what is happening)
Mi waah fi explore an si if mi can mek it tap
(I want to make it stop)
But mi want it more
(but I want more)
Mi want it suh bad till it all feel wrong
(The depth of my longing for this seems wrong)

An mi brain til ah talk tuh mi
(My brain is still speaking)
An it ah confuse mi baad
(and i'm so confused)
Cause mi til nuh undastan what a gwaan
(I still don't get it)
Mi nuh know ah wah mi ah feel
(I still don't know what is this im feeling)
Or which pawt ah mi should be feelin dis ting
(should I feel this in only a part or all of me)

Mi brain seh, Toes, curl up
(my brain tells my toes to curl up)
An mi toe dem curl up til mi all get ah muscle contrac
(and my toes curl and I get a muscle contract)
An I feel dat ting yuh si
(and I feel it so bad)
(di muscle contract dat is
(the feel the muscle contract)
But inna di migle of all ah dat
(but in the middle of this situation)
Dis ting, dis feelin
(this thing, this feeling)

A ride mi; confuse mi
(its riding and confusing me)
Cause mi neva feel nuttin like dis before inna my life
(because I've never felt anything like this before)

But yuh si mi dying trial
(Can you imagine)
Ah wah dis
(what is this)
How dis jus a tun mi inna idiot suh
(This make me feel silly)
Is jus a touch
(it was just a touch)
But it a mek mi belly flutta
(but it makes my stomach flutter)
An mi hawt a beat
(my hearts beating fast)
Mi hair dem tan up
(my hairs are risen)
Mi toe dem curl up
(my toes are curled)
Mi all get muscle contract
(I even got a muscle contract)
An mi finga tip dem ah tingle
(my fingers are tingling)
Mi mout a drip water
(my mouth is watering)
And did I mention
Dat mi ah hear betta
(That i'm hearing better)
An smell, nuh mek mi guh dey suh
(and smell, let's not go there)

Mi dear me smell someting
(I smell something)
It mek mi close mi eye dem
(it makes me close my eyes)
An mi imagination gaan wid it

(my imagination takes over)
Blowse and skirt…ah wah mi si
(Wait a minute, what is that)
Nuh one man
(is that a man)
Him beautiful yuh si
(he's so beautiful)
Mi virtual reality
(my virtual reality)
Mek mi conscious
(makes me conscious)
Fi si seh only when mi eye dem close
(that only when my spirit is open to him)
Mi si him face to face
(I see him)
An mi hear im voice
(and head him speak)
Dat silky smood, peaceful voice
(That still small voice)
An when mi open my eye dem
(and when I realize)
Mi know sey a di spirit of God mi feel
(I know im experiencing the presence of God)
All chroo fi touch
(Because the holy ghost touched my life).

This Is Me

Used
Me
Tired
Me
Do this
Me
Do that
Me
Be there
Me
Always ready
Me
Anytime
Me

Shoulders broad and drenched with somebody else's tears
Being that my tear ducts are blocked by the fact that my heart is blue black
from shattering words
And inveterate actions of those friends, associates, even my family. Me.

Loving
Me
Caring
Me
Aimable
Me
Wanting the best for others and everybody else
Me

Forgotten cause im always visible
Right in your face
Im there but not there
And when I, really no there, im seen
Im MIA (missing in action)
And NAMP (not at my post)
Because I was sick and tired and burned out and overwhelmed and used
and hurt and angry and forgotten

Even I forgot
Me
Who?
Me
Silent
Me
Sweet
Me
What happened?
Why?
Me
Send
Me
Cause I hear You calling
Me
And even though I feel I can't make it I still want to go

Stupid
Me
Get better; try harder
I gotta make it
Can't get comfortable
Pissed off
Going in circles
Me
A fanatic for life
Me
But dying
Me

Bad habits; funky desires
Praise and glory – my supposed defenses
Me.

Striving
Me
How
Me
Why
Me
Live
Me
Destined
Me

Change
Me
Where did that come from?
What did I just say?
Yes
Change, me
I know it will hurt cause that's usually what change does
From bad to good
And good to better
But I must deny me
So still I say
Change
Me
Through the hurt, through the trials, the storms, the mountains, the valleys,
the joys, the cries, the blindness, the wilderness, the loss
Loss of who?
Me
For YOU
Your birth, my death
And I live
Me

You want me to say I can make it
I can go on
And even though my mind and my heart says two different things
I muster up the courage and say – I Can!

So hard is my back that when pressures come
I will stand against the grain in your strength
Yes, me
And plastic is my face that when tears fall
They'll stream down and rest upon my chest – a fertile place and be the
Subliminal hindrances and intended treatments for my growth
My fertilizing situations and irrigation systems
My destiny building resources

Yes, me
I'll take it
Me
I'll work it
Me
I'll use it
Me
I'll make it
Me
Yes, me

I will live
And not die
Yes, me
I will scream it to the mountain top
I will survive, and rise
Yes, me
I will fight and run
I will win
Me

Impulse Happens

So, you need a tension release
And you say only I can give it.
My kiss takes you to places where problems can't touch you.

You float on air
Your insides relax
You breathe better
All from my kiss

Now who wouldn't be flattered by that?
But it's not flattery that made me do it.

I wanted to relax you
I wanted to relax me

It started with. Hug
Then a cheek rub
Then a cheek peck

Then I made a big mistake
I looked in your eyes
Your heart peeked out and captured me

Next thing I knew
I was falling into such softness
My heart fluttered to life
Memories kicked in
Feelings sunk in and I was lost

Our lips have never forgotten each other it seems
I don't know anything right now
I'm so light I don't know how I'm still touching ground
My head is tight and full, and I can't breathe, and I can't see, and I remember
what you used to do to me

So, hours past and we just got started
And I'm hot and I have to pull away
Or else I won't be able to tell where I start and where you end
And I have to stop this because I want it all
And neither one of us can have it all

And where was I again?
More time is gone, or did it stop?
I don't know
What
Just
Happened

Repentance Answers

Succulence
Sweet
Deadly
Innocence
Experienced
A solution to a problem
You think
Let it be
Where the heart lies

Suffocated desires
Relentless love
A need
A want
An escape
To a place know to us both
Together while apart
Laughter without sound
Expressed with the exhilaration of your heartbeat
Smiles to your mind
A cloud so real it's unattainable
A place where things happen
And words can't be spoken

You act
You move
You run
You walk
You sigh

You cry
You live
For the moment
Of memory
And the fulfillment of it all
True but not your reality

You let go
Surrendered
To mistake and fear
You allowed it and relaxed
And slept awake
Filled with emotion and sensuality
It was good but not right
It was umami but costly
It shouldn't have
But it did
Inhibited
It held you captive without chains

but now
Sanctioned
Atoned
Bought
Paid for
Repented
Changed
Blood red flows deep
Forgiven
Redeemed
So what?
Impulse happened
Fruit of the spirit is now being developed
Move
You died last night
Today
You live!

Orgasm

Catch me when I fall
Right before my face gets to the place
Of piercing and tumultuous pain
Where crimson flows and white flesh shows

Take me up out of grime
Take me to your place right in the nick of time
The nick of my time but your right time

Shed from me the old
Old skin that breaks and blemishes
And replace on me, in me, thru me,
The new wine, new hair, new skin,
New beauty of you.

Let the shine be like that of coal burned and chipped at
Bringing forth something I once couldn't afford
Let me be the rarest let me be the finest
Let me be the biggest of your eye
Your diamond with all its C's
A diamond with all your characters naturality

Rub me, slowly
Let me feel your caress
Your hands upon me
Your duly press

Arouse my intellect
Heighten my senses
Glorify my spirituality and love me
Let me love me
Let me love you
Love you till eternity

Shine I say
Glow I say
Resurrect within me
A light, a love, a glow
I just don't know
A place that if on my own
I just couldn't reach
The pinnacle of my – coming
Yes, oh yes, I say
I'm coming into your glory

Oh my God, this is sweet
Finally, a fantasy that blows my mind to pieces

Unknown totally without control
For you've got it
You turn it up or down
Sometimes even around
You can ring it, swing it,
Let it flow just the way you know
just the way you like

You can have me
You can use me
You can love me
Yu can share me
You can change me
Rearrange me into your beauty
A climax of change
I'm ready for my ministry

So, I say, preach on sista
Press on girl
Trust in your lover
Your master
Your brother
Your sista
Your friend
Your lord and savior, Amen

Nah man, Take it back
What was yours, take it back
What is yours, take it back
What is now to be, your ministry

And flow with The One who aint neva hurt you…
When he penetrated
Flow with The One
Who aint neva made you cry - for sadness
Flow with the One
Who aint neva left you alone
Or forgot you when the winds blew hard, real hard
But who held you (you just couldn't feel it)
Who carried you (you just had the wrong frame of mind – at that time)
When he was on you

But now you're in Him and He's all in you
And together there is nothing that you both as one can't do
Just let Him be sista
Just follow the cross
Just watch them footprints
That only you can see
And walk into your out-of-this-world destiny
Walk into YOUR MINISTRY!

Cultured Sweetness

I love being black
I just love who I am
I love my hair
Even though the comb touches it and it takes a minute to comb through
And when it does it hurts real bad because it go stuck in what you would
call my 'nigga naps'

I love my smile
I love my laugh
Even though my teeth are crooked
i have a gap
and my mother can't afford to send me to the dentist because the copay is
high, and my father just got laid off
This black, sweetened, smooth, scorned by many skin – my black skin

I love my family
My two sisters, three brothers, my cousin who lives with us cause her
momma left her for the john up the street; my 70 year old-glaucoma in
one eye uncle who lives with us because it's cheaper than putting him up
in some low down dilapidated – considered (5 Star) – for people like me –
nursing home.
And then there are the many others near and far
And just because my sisters and brothers are lighter than me and *my daddy*
is as dark as night, and we live in a three bedroom apartment, that don't
mean nothin.

We family.
I love our blend
Like a good cup of cramping cup of red kool aid with just the right amount
of sugar

I love the way we cook
The heart and soul of the matter
The food – it keeps us together

My mom does all kinds of cooking

Like fried chicken (which taste better the next day)
Or fried fish with a nice warm slice of hard dough bread with some butter
(that's the west Indian part of me)
Then there is the rice and beans and smothered chicken
I like the veggies too
I eat them because it keeps my mom happy

I love my life
I love he stories my dad tells us when we sit together
Yea, sit together and not because something went wrong, or Jeff (that's my
brother) got in trouble, or we suddenly had to move
It is just to tell stories
Just to talk
Just to tell us where we come from
Just to tell us bout my great, great grandmama and granddaddy, and other
family that had died and gone
'bout the journey they took (and actually made it), the obstacles they faced,
the cotton they picked, the whips they pick for their own benefit
(if you get what I mean)
Just to tell us how strong we are
How much they love us
How much we are somebody
So, I can be anything I want to be

I love my back
My broad back
My brute strength
And that's it.
I love this skin
This skin I'm in
I love my life
I love being black
It is essence
I love me!

Free

Me – I wanna be free
I must be free
Free from my inner slavery
My soul of memories
And hurts and pains
My real and unreal subconscious mysteries
You know, the problems I know I have and the ones I pretend I don't.

Separation to be free; separation from even me
From:
F – fraudulence (faking the funk and player hating *to faithfulness* – to my lover
R – reasonable (when I feel like it *to righteousness* – everyday living
E – elimination (being sifted like wheat *to elevation* – rising from glory to glory
E – ecstasy (which last me but for a minute *to eternity* - life forever
Totally FREE

Smiling, showing teeth as white as His robe
Thinking the thoughts not His but within His image
Laughing, now that I can
And my praise that is filled with glorious exaltations
Ringing forth with melodies sweet
In my song of triumphant jubilee
Saying, "I'm FREE, free from my inner slavery".

No more!
No more of the was, and the why
No more of the how come and the it's not fair
No more worries and tears
But if tears must fall it's because
A bound woman has become free
That free woman is me!

The Art of Coming

Just talks about accepting self…
So much of a struggle to accept the invisible and hold onto the promise of me
So long I walked in the shoes of ancestors
Enlisting and holding proudly the stories of their captivity
Though I should stand on the shoulders of their strength
It's always been easier to just give; relinquish my identity to the past of their
struggle instead of trying to find me.

It's in the books if you step on concrete paths that lead to HBCUs
and the stories on Sundays from the verandas, and patios, and porches;
From the rooms with the plastic on the couches.
It's on the tube, resounding names like Martin and X
Who fought not just flexed and created parts of history that gave hope and
fight.

With not much changing for the black in a white world, would it be easier
to find myself in my color, my race or to find myself in the Creator and
this new life I've gained?
It doesn't take away my humanness and that by whicI'm acknowledged in
this world, but who am I and am I becoming?

Hate fills the air. Injustice plagues our world. Racism breathes heavily. *And
yet I hear, Love covers a multitude of sin.*
I'm torn to become when I'm trying to see what I should become and
according to whom.

There is a fight to love when Garner... the chokehold, his last words...I can't breathe... plays virtually in a loop
What about Parker in California... the father of five
Unarmed but tased repeatedly.
How about the friends who were to be there just like they said they would?
And there is the neighbor friend who lived with us but, but they were never there and abandoned me or the family that was not family but took a piece of me - the greatest part of me.

One song writer said, what the world needs now, is love sweet love, it's the only thing that there's just too little of."
Ain't that the truth?

John said love was so great
that that's how God exhibited love.
He did everything for us.
He offered His beloved Son to save us.
Jesus died and waged the price.

It wasn't like the others - our brothers and sisters
who through injustice and against their will
were unlawfully detained and insolently assassinated.
You nor I did they have on their minds
All they wanted was just to stay alive.

This execution was of his own recognizance
in a time when this was the norm
he for some crazy reason
had me and you on his mind.
What manner of love is this
that he would choose
to save a bloody sucker like me?

Doctors had a diagnosis
for the bloody sweat
called hematidrosis that gushed from his side.
Physical trauma

battered and bruised
dehydrated and exhausted
Spat upon, cussed out and abused.

For me he died.

Emotional and mental stress,
sadistic sport – blindfolding him, taunting him
unrecognizable mass of torn bleeding tissue
body flaccidly hanging
intermittent partial asphyxiation
yet still he said, Father forgive them
for they know not what they do.
Me and you
consumed his heart
and he said, It is finished.

Gimme a second I can't breathe
he's been better than good to me

Then soon He rose again
with all power in his hand
dumbfounding the wise
overwhelming his friends

making a way before a way was needed
loosing my shackles before I was captive
healing my body before I became sick
keeping my mind before I lost it

I think he loves me.

no one else had the privilege
nor the power to cover me
choosing to die for me, but HE did.
He rose again.

Not only was the travesty complete
but access to live became available
I said yes and I started to come.
He knew me, he found me, I accepted him.

This coming is to the knowledge of who HE is
I am here.

My Essential Thing

I am compelled to lay down
compelled to fall down
compelled to bow down

compelled to let down
Hmmm

God
your presence takes me from a quandary
Makes me do my soul's laundry (hahaha)
I don't want to be nasty
cuz your presence wants me, holy
wants me solely
doesn't want to share me
you

You want me only
Mmm, yeah

You see everywhere I'm going
everybody can't go
sometimes it's so lonely
terrifying and makes me queasy
but

I want you

You hold me so close
and breathe into me with your kiss
You remove from me the six by eight cell mentality
filled with my experiences
and jacked up memories
and you give me RE-VI-VAL

Your fire is falling
It's falling down on me

My eyes gaze to the hills
and your presence feels me
You make me still
lay me down in green pastures
You settle me

And there, My soul, dies
cause I get to see you more
I'm alive (hold it out with excitement)

What is it about you that makes me cry when I'm happy?
What is it about you that makes me laugh when I'm sad?
What is about you that makes me help somebody when my things are hard -
share my testimony?

You make me go haaaarrd
your presence is my rewaaaarrd

You are my pusher
essential to my livelihood
giving me unction to function

One Friday in february over thirty years ago
You laid your hand on me
Reminded me that from the womb
You had a name,
you had a call,

you had a purpose for me
You weighed in heavy on me

And like a criminal on the run
I was caught
You arrested my heart
I surrendered my soul

And you did something to me.

What is man that you are conscious of him?
You in me, and I am conscious of you,
And me, and us, and this, and that, and prophecy, and back then and now
and tomorrow
I don't…
My mind is blown
but your voice bellows though it's a whisper
and I moan as you speak
cause I feel the tremor in the power of your word
and it's real, oh I can feel it in my soul

God, what have you done to me?

Your peace subdues me
in spite of all the crazy
It's more powerful than man's most powerful
more aggressive than COVID19
more potent than prozac
More effective than special k
More settling than lithium

Your peace
your presence
Intensifies my feelings
overloads my sensory experiences
and while it's not emotionalism

I feel you

I know you're there;
you're Here
God… you're right here
you're everywhere

You impact my thought
You affect my mood
You shift my behavior
and with glorious exaltations
I get stupid for you

You increase my heart rate
Instead of loss, my memory is restored
Cause I'm thinking of your grace,
I'm remembering that it was you,
it's been you
It's always been you

Instead of feeling pain
you give me fullness of joy
and pleasures I can't explain
You make me forgive the men who raped me
You make love flow from a place
that just dumbfounds me

You make me multilingual
You commune with me on another level
I'm able to tell you encrypted messages
Like kabasatabalamahanatala
And only you know what i mean

My spirit to your spirit
bypassing the understanding of men
annihilating satan's plan

Engaging the ears of the heavens -
they open up
You respond - to me
and angels attend to my voice

You remove anxiety and make me rest for a while

I crave you, sweat for you, need you, die daily for you
I must continually ingest you
The true, the good, the pure, the just, the virtuous, the praise worthy, the
honest

My need for you is chronic

Without you I may be harmful, unpleasant uncontrollable and hypocritical
But Your presence makes me
and without you I am nothing

Who is like you?

I am overwhelmed by you
You make me quiver in every area
it's sacrilegious
but your touch
your presence
your word

it amazes me as I contemplate my testimonies
my triumphs, the deliverances
your gifts, the birthing in my spirit -
the pushing of my purpose and voila...

I give you permission to come
I have come...Here
We are
Alone in a crowded room
It's just me and you

Again, here I am
On the floor face down cause
Your presence makes - me - lie - down
I am humbled that you want to be with me
go away with me

from the articulation of Solomon the king,
I am your Beloved
and you are my essential thing.

www.ingramcontent.com/pod-product-compliance
Lightning Source LLC
Chambersburg PA
CBHW020844150726
48196CB00002B/219